With love

To

From

Girlfriends

new seasons™

Picture credits:

Front cover (inset): **Orion Press/Natural Selections**
Book jacket illustrated by Robin Moro.
Art Resource: © 2003 Estate of Pablo Picasso/Artists Rights Society (ARS), New York/Réunion des Musées Nationaux; Erich Lessing; **Sharon K. Broutzas;** © **Corbis:** The Barnes Foundation, Merion Station; Christie's Images; Randy Faris; Louis K. Meisel Gallery; LWA-Stephen Welstead; Philadelphia Museum of Art; **Joyce Shelton; SuperStock:** Christie's Images; Gallery Contemporanea; The Grand Design; Kactus Foto; Hyacinth Manning-Carner; Daniel Nevins; Peter Sickles; Peter Willi

Contributing writers:

Elaine Creasman, Lain Chroust Ehmann, Jan Goldberg, Jennifer Ouellette
Other quotes compiled by Joan Loshek.

Acknowledgments:

Publications International, Ltd., has made every effort to locate the owners of all copyrighted material to obtain permission to use the selections that appear in this book. Any errors or omissions are unintentional; corrections, if necessary, will be made in future editions.

Excerpt from *Women Make the Best Friends: A Celebration* by Lois Wyse. Copyright © 1995 by Lois Wyse. Reprinted by permission of William Morris Agency, Inc., on behalf of author.

Excerpt by Judy Lane from *Girlfriends for Life: Friendships Worth Keeping Forever.* Copyright © 1998 by Carmen Renee Berry and Tamara C. Traeder. Reprinted with permission from Wildcat Canyon Press, a division of Circulus Publishing Group, Inc., Berkeley, CA. All rights reserved.

Excerpt by Aimee Olivo from *Girlfriends for Life: Friendships Worth Keeping Forever.* Copyright © 1998 by Carmen Renee Berry and Tamara C. Traeder. Reprinted with permission from Wildcat Canyon Press, a division of Circulus Publishing Group, Inc., Berkeley, CA. All rights reserved.

The door to a friend's heart (and closet!) is always open.

*I*t's easy for me to soar
with our friendship
as a safety net.

My best
girlfriend helps
me hold on
and hang in.

Our Photo

Girlfriends mean the difference
between an ordinary event and an
extraordinary event.

*I*t's not important how girlfriends met or where they came from; it's the places they go together that matter.

Girlfriends hear what you mean rather than what you say.

*H*ave you ever noticed that
the longer we talk on the phone,
the shorter the call feels?

...if you have just one
person with whom you
can be weak, miserable
and contrite, and who
won't hurt you for it, then
you are rich.

MARGARETE BUBER-NEUMANN, *MILENA*

I'm only as good
(or as bad) as my
girlfriends.

Girlfriends are the ones you laugh with until tears are streaming down your face, and then you wonder together what was so funny.

With girlfriends
like you,
who needs
chocolate?

When I see *that look* on your face

I want to *laugh, cry*, and *hug* you 'til it hurts...

YOU UNDERSTAND!

*Y*our simple nod
gives me all the
confidence I need.

Good friends are like a great pair of shoes:
They're comfortable, they come in all sizes, and
they make you feel good about yourself!

*B*elieving in this
friendship
is a no-brainer.

Finding a true friend
is like striking it rich
with the real thing
in a river teeming
with fool's gold.

God gives us our relatives—
thank God we can choose
our friends.

ETHEL WATTS MUMFORD

Feel free to count on me—
I'll always be here.

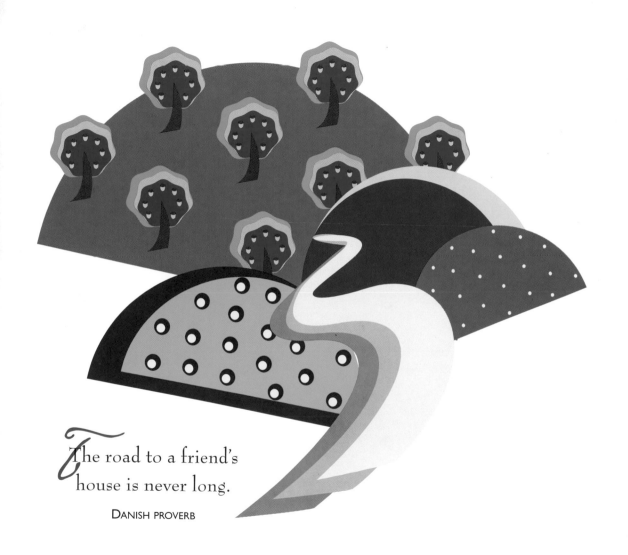

The road to a friend's house is never long.

DANISH PROVERB

Girlfriends offer the wonderful gift of perspective.

When this world is depressing
and my problems are distressing,
Girlfriend, you are there—
what a blessing!

She is forever doing things that
bring huge smiles to my face.

AIMEE OLIVO

Our Photo

With girlfriends
we dare to be
who we really are.

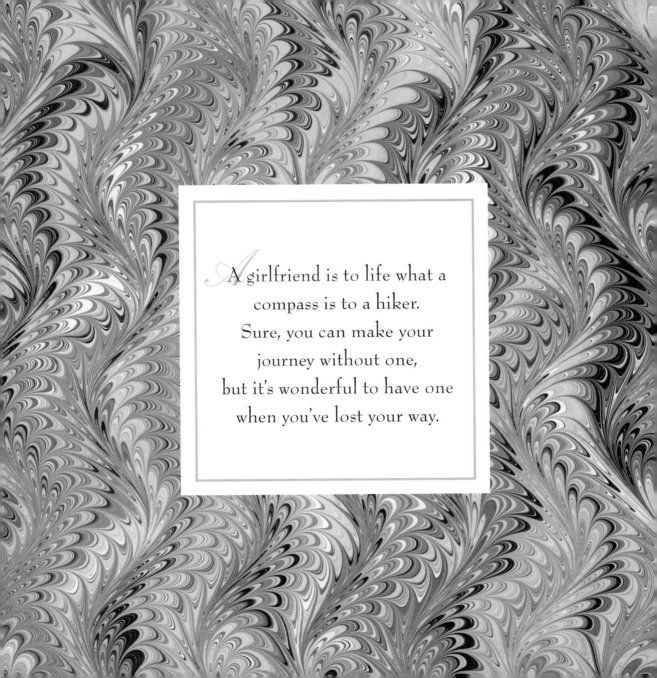

A girlfriend is to life what a compass is to a hiker. Sure, you can make your journey without one, but it's wonderful to have one when you've lost your way.

Although you often know a faster path, you're always willing to walk a bit longer to keep me company.

No matter how much you whine,
complain, or vent, a girlfriend
always calls the next day.

$\mathcal{A}$lthough some of your pep talks have worked better than others, thanks for always being my biggest cheerleader.

A real friend

never gets in your way—

unless you HAPPEN

to be on your way DOWN.

ANONYMOUS

Every moment

with you feels

like a gift.

*G*irlfriends are like chocolate, automatic
transmissions, and indoor plumbing.
We only know how much we need them
when we try to live without them!

It's the ones you can call up at 4:00 A.M. that matter.

MARLENE DIETRICH, IN *POPCORN IN PARADISE*

The best mirror is an old friend.

GEORGE HERBERT

$\mathcal{I}$ am grateful for someone who understands when the whole world doesn't.

JUDY LANE

Age doesn't matter when it comes to girlfriends.

Unless, of course,

that age looks better on her than it does on you.

At our first concert we
bought each other T-shirts.
Today, we'd buy each other
earplugs. Rock on, girlfriend!

*O*nly your real friends
tell you when your face
is dirty.

SICILIAN PROVERB

Girlfriends are like Champagne—they add an effervescence that makes any event more special.

Sometimes I think you know way too much about me.
Now we'll have to be friends forever!

Our Photo

Your girlfriend always
remembers your birthday—
even though she has
conveniently forgotten
your age.

Some people move our souls to dance.

UNKNOWN

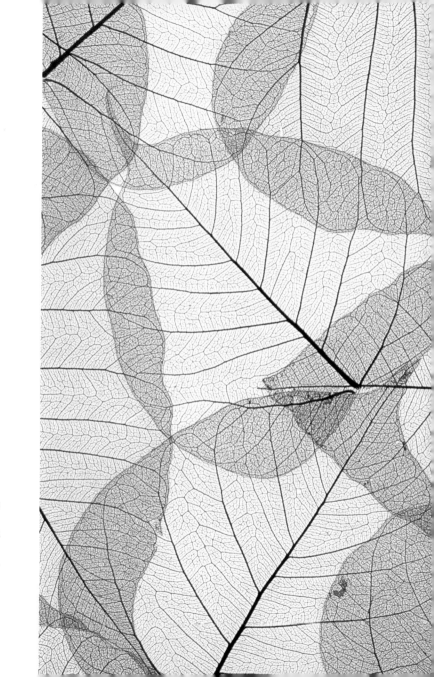

The magic of true
friendship weaves a
spell that never ends.

How lucky I am to have
known someone who was so
hard to say goodbye to.

UNKNOWN

Girlfriends can have an
entire conversation without
ever saying a word.

If you have one true friend,
you have more than your share.

THOMAS FULLER

*T*rue friends don't grow apart;
they grow old...together.

A good friend is . . . the
key to sanity in a
totally insane world.

LOIS WYSE

If all my friends were to jump off a bridge, I would not follow. I would be at the bottom to catch them when they fall.

UNKNOWN

The bright light of our friendship
guides me through the dark.

We've been through so much together, it's sometimes hard to remember where my experiences end and yours begin!

Even when I'm laughing so
hard I can't make it past
"Remember the time..." you
already know exactly what
I'm talking about and are
laughing right along with me.

Our Photo

I can count on my girlfriends for everything—from an emergency safety pin to a middle-of-the-night pep talk.

An honest answer is the sign of true friendship.

Bad haircuts,
broken hearts, braces—
your best friend has seen
you through it all.
Though you may be older
and your problems more
complicated,
a friendly ear is still
often the best cure.

A real friend will help you forget the things you don't want to remember.

*H*Here's to many future
adventures together!